This Pet Journal belongs to

_____

_____

Pet Photo

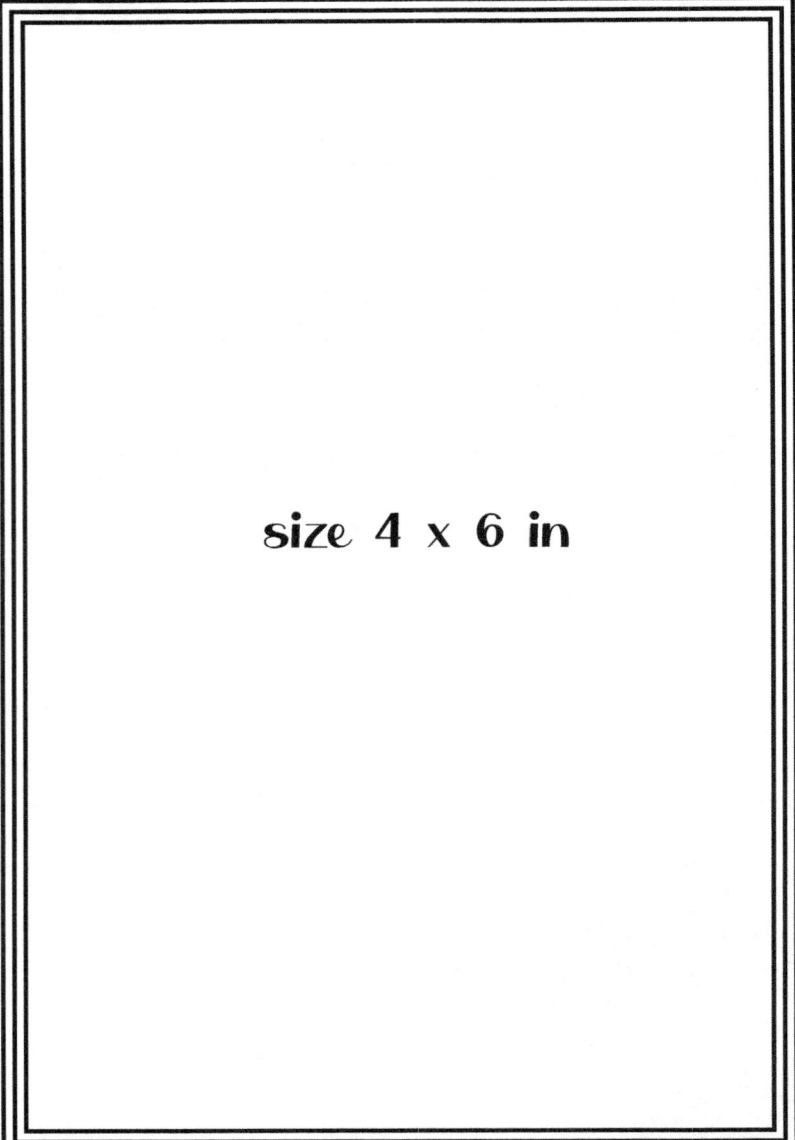

Pet Profile

Pet Name:

Sex:

Color:

Birthday:

Breed:

Microchip info.

Medical condition

Personality traits

Habits

Vaccinations

Date	Weight	Against

Emergency contacts

Name	Phone

Daily Log

Daily Log

Daily Log

Daily Log

Vet Visits

Date	Purpose	Clinic name

Daily Log

Daily Log

Daily Log

Daily Log

Daily Log

Daily Log

Daily Log

Daily Log

Daily Log

Daily Log

Daily Log

Daily Log

Daily Log

Daily Log

Daily Log

Daily Log

Daily Log

Daily Log

Daily Log

Daily Log

Daily Log

Daily Log

Daily Log

Daily Log

Daily Log

Daily Log

Daily Log

Daily Log

Daily Log

Daily Log

Daily Log

Daily Log

Daily Log

Daily Log

Daily Log

Daily Log

Daily Log

Daily Log

Daily Log

Daily Log

Daily Log

Daily Log

Daily Log

Daily Log

Daily Log

Daily Log

Daily Log

Daily Log

Daily Log

Daily Log

Daily Log

Daily Log

Daily Log

Daily Log

Daily Log

Daily Log

Daily Log

Daily Log

Daily Log

Daily Log

Daily Log

Daily Log

Daily Log

Daily Log

Daily Log

Daily Log

Daily Log

Daily Log

Daily Log

Daily Log

Daily Log

Daily Log

Daily Log

Daily Log

Daily Log

Daily Log

Daily Log

Daily Log

Daily Log

Daily Log

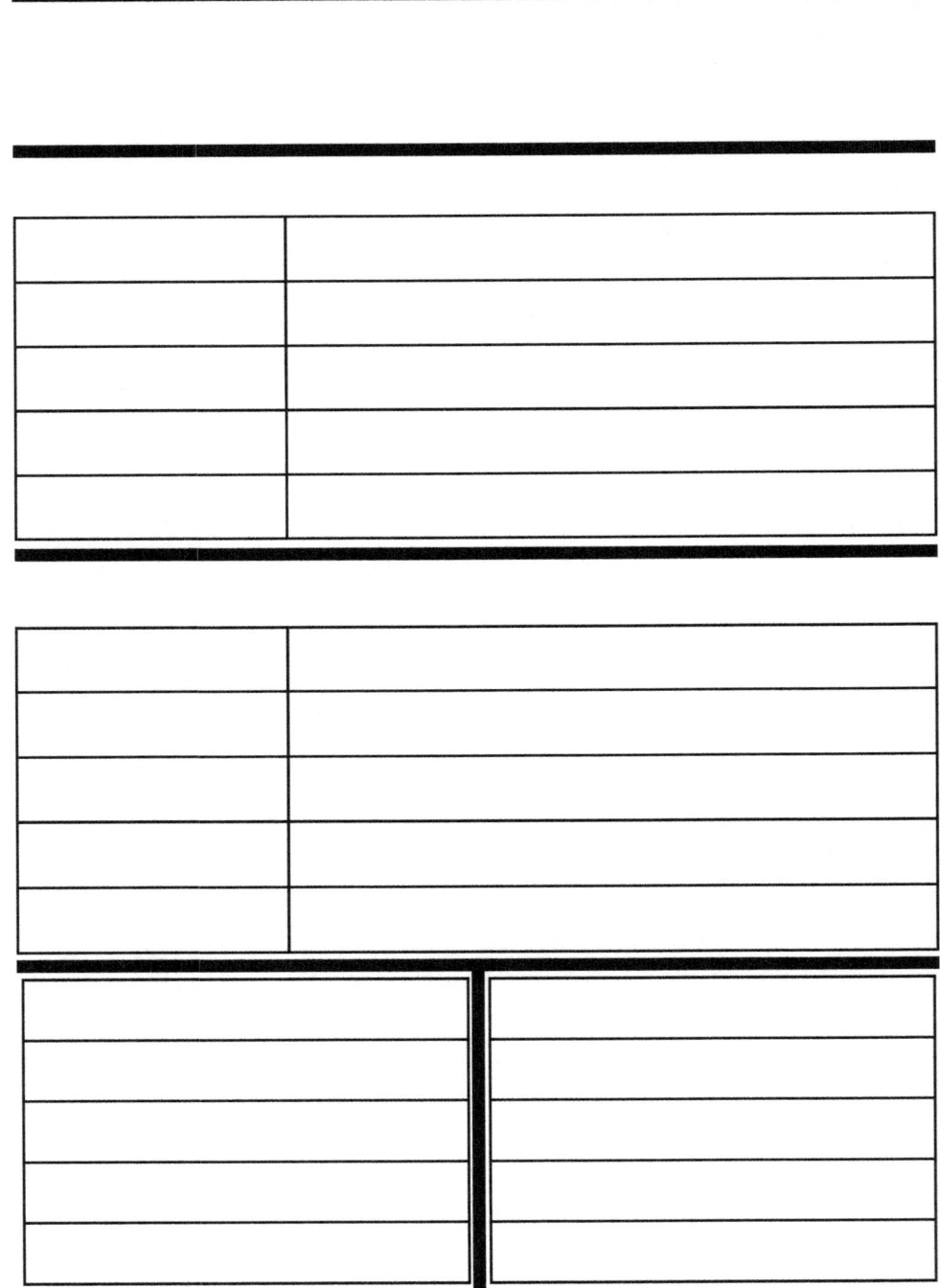

Daily Log

Daily Log

Daily Log

Daily Log

Daily Log

Daily Log

Daily Log

Printed in Great Britain
by Amazon